PUT THE CAT IN THE OVEN BEFORE YOU DESCRIBE THE KITCHEN

JAKE VANDER ARK

D0109935

PUT THE CAT IN THE OVEN
BEFORE YOU DESCRIBE THE KITCHEN

Third Edition: October, 2017

ISBN: 978-1977718051

www.jakevanderark.com
jake.vander.ark@gmail.com

Cover design by Jake Vander Ark
Author photo by Susannah Bailey

PRAISE FOR CAT

INTRODUCTION

There are a few things you should know before we jump in:

I hate filler in how-to books... especially long introductions.

Sometimes I capitalize words for emphasis. Don't do this.

This book contains many lessons I devised while writing my own novels. It also includes classic tips from better writers, selected for their usefulness, then distilled into bite-sized nuggets for easy learning.

I'm a movie and TV nerd. This will be obvious in several of the examples I use throughout this book. Since it's faster to watch a movie than to read a novel, I thought this would be an easy way for beginners to study the craft. This also means that most the of the tips can be applied to screenwriting as well!

I tend to walk the line between mainstream and literary fiction. In general, mainstream focuses on plot while literary focuses on character. Instead of choosing between the two, I emphasize the need for both. Hopefully writers from both genres will find value in these lessons.

If you have questions about a tip or suggestions for later editions, please let me know at jake.vander.ark@gmail.com. I hope to update this book regularly, and the ebook version will always be free.

This book moves quickly from adorable tips to soul-crushing life lessons, so buckle up!

EXTREMELY SIMPLE TIPS

THE NUMBER ONE RULE:
SHOW, DON'T TELL

This is the greatest trick to get the reader involved in your story. If you can master this one technique, then grammar, character, and description will matter less.

Yep, you read that right: This rule is more important than grammar, character, or description.

Consider this opening paragraph:

My name is Kennedy. I'm fourteen. I live with my mom. Oh, and by the way, I think I'm turning into a werewolf!

This is a classic example of TELLING rather than SHOWING. We don't get to experience Kennedy's pain of being a werewolf... and hell, we don't have any reason to believe her!

So the million-dollar question is this: How do we SHOW these things instead?

The first step is to open the scene *in the moment*. Start with action or dialogue that draws the reader into the story and SHOWS them the important details in real time as if it's happening right now.

Consider this rewrite:

I'm no expert on the human body, but I'm pretty sure fourteen-year-old girls aren't supposed to grow fur on their kneecaps.

I slammed my bedroom door, plopped on my bed, and slipped my jeans to my ankles. Sure enough, the fur was back. What the heck? *I thought and examined my legs closer. It was black this time instead of grey.*

"Kennedy! Get your butt in the kitchen!" Mom had the worst timing.

"Just a minute, Ma!" I called, then snatched a pair of scissors from my nightstand. Carefully, I snipped away at the patch of fuzz and prayed to God it wasn't growing in a place my mother could see.

"Kennedy? The dishes aren't going to clean themselves!"

I gathered the clump of hair, ran to my dresser, and opened the top drawer. It was filled from top to bottom with fur. I crammed in the new clump, slammed the drawer, and bolted from my room.

This paragraph will engage readers AND hit the important points. We know the girl's name is Kennedy because her mom calls her to the kitchen. We know she's a werewolf because she's cutting fur from her knee.

Try to find places in your own writing where you can show rather than tell. I promise, it'll make all the difference in the world.

THERE'S NO SHAME IN SIMPLE LANGUAGE

The first tip was the most important. The second is the easiest.

Write simply.

New wordsmiths often assail their introductory tome with a thesaurus merely a mouse-click away. They presuppose that enormous or ostentatious words will make them seem more intellectual. Instead, colossal words can make them sound highfalutin, add unintended denotation to their story, and decelerate the reader's pace.

Let's try that again.

New writers often attack their first book with a thesaurus only a mouse-click away. They presume large or showy words will make them sound smarter. Instead, big words can make them sound pretentious, add unintended meaning to their story, and slow down the reader.

"Simple language" also includes the amount of syllables in a word. In the above example, I replaced the word "enormous" with "large" simply because "large" has fewer syllables and makes the sentence easier to read.

If you're not using the word in your day-to-day conversations, it might be difficult to use it properly in your book. If you can say it with a simpler word, use the simpler word!

FIND ORIGINAL IDEAS
IN UNORIGINAL STORIES

The fact is, nobody will ever write an original idea. EVERYTHING has been done before.

However, we can search for details about our stories that will make them stand out from the rest. If you're writing a vampire story, try changing the classic vampire rules. From what I'm told, the *Twilight* vampires twinkle (or something). This detail is a new addition that Stephenie Meyer created to distinguish her story from the all the other vampire fiction. And it works!

Here's a trick that works for me. Try combining two big ideas into one. Do you have a vampire story that needs to be spiced up? Set it in a nursing home. Or maybe you need a vampire with an original struggle. What if he likes girls, but can only live off the blood of other boys?

This tip is essential in the teen romance genre. You will never write a unique story about teens falling in love, but if you find little ways to make your story stand out, you can go a long way in keeping the reader's attention.

WHEN DESCRIBING PEOPLE, TELL US WHAT MAKES THEM DIFFERENT

How many times have you read this sentence?

Dylan had blonde hair that hung just past his blue eyes.

Dylan ALWAYS has blonde, brown, or black hair, blue or piercing-green eyes, and a well-sculpted body. And so does everyone else! Not only is Dylan unoriginal, he's totally forgettable. When Samantha is searching through a sea of young men for "Mr. Right," we need some distinctions.

Try mixing things up. Maybe Dylan has a scar on his right cheek; not big enough to be ugly, just big enough to make him a badass. Maybe he has a tattoo of a humming bird on his left bicep. Maybe his stylist slipped with the scissors and his hair is a bit lopsided (which, of course, doesn't take away from the speck of brown in his gorgeous green eyes).

Want to go farther? Give your characters *(gasp)* imperfections. Give us a boy with chubby hands or a girl with a gap in her teeth.

For stories with lots of characters, these distinctions aren't just interesting, they're vital to help your reader remember who's who!

WATCH OUT FOR
BACKWARDS SENTENCES

A backwards sentence has the ability to strip the power and flow from your writing. Scan your story for sentences with a comma right in the middle. Most of the time it can be flipped for a cleaner read.

Dashing through the field, Liam leapt for joy. Watching the setting sun, he felt a tremendous sense of peace.

Let's flip both sentences:

Liam leapt for joy as he dashed through the field. He felt a tremendous sense of peace as he watched the setting sun.

There are times when a backwards sentence is the better choice, but four out of five times, straightforward is better.

DON'T LET "WAS" SLOW
YOU DOWN

Look at the first few words of your sentence. Is the word "was" in there? What about "were?"

"Was" and "were" will destroy your sentences. They make the action sound as if it already happened, and this will make your reader feel like they're HEARING about your story instead of LIVING it. Too many "was"s and "were"s will make your book drag.

Luckily, there's an easy way to fix this: ACTION words.

Check out this paragraph from *The Accidental Siren*:

The water tower was dark and terrible above our heads. Brambles were tugging at our skin and branches were hunting our vulnerable eyes. The storm was over us, wailing like a hundred dying cats, splitting the sky with silver streaks and threatening to finish us off. Mara was leading me south. Minutes later we were out of the woods.

To make this paragraph more exciting, let's replace "was" and "were" with action words.

The water tower loomed dark and terrible above our heads. Brambles tugged at our skin and branches hunted our vulnerable eyes. The storm overtook us, wailing like a hundred dying cats, splitting the sky with silver streaks and threatening to finish us off. Mara led me south. Minutes later we emerged from the woods.

The best part about action words is that they add description without making your story longer. *"The water tower WAS over our heads." "The water tower LOOMED over our heads."* Both sentences have the same amount of words—the same amount of syllables, even—but the second one is far more intriguing!

PUT THE CAT IN THE OVEN BEFORE YOU DESCRIBE THE KITCHEN

Yes, I made that up. And yeah, it's disturbing. But it's a vital trick to learn, especially at the beginning of your book!

What do you think about these opening paragraphs?

Hunter's kitchen had countertops that seemed perpetually smeared with grease. The floor was yellow linoleum with rust marks from the ancient refrigerator that smelled like banana peels, rotten cheese, and piss. A ceiling fan sucked steam from the kettle on the neon coils of an electric stove.

Hunter stooped to his knees. "Sprinkles!" he said and clapped his hands. "Here kitty, kitty!"

The cat came charging into the kitchen. Hunter snatched him up, opened the oven, set the dial to 400 degrees, and tossed the kitten inside.

The action in these paragraphs has the potential to grip a reader's attention. Unfortunately, it comes too late! Nobody wants to pick up a book and read about a kitchen.

Check out the difference. And be sure to reread the whole paragraph to see the effect.

Hunter stooped to his knees. "Sprinkles!" he said and clapped his hands. "Here kitty, kitty!"

The cat charged into the kitchen. Hunter snatched him up, opened the oven, set the dial to 400 degrees, and tossed the kitten inside.

Hunter's kitchen had countertops that seemed perpetually smeared with grease. The floor was yellow linoleum with rust marks from the ancient refrigerator that smelled like banana peels, rotten cheese, and piss. A ceiling fan sucked steam from the kettle on the neon coils of an electric stove.

See what happens when the description comes AFTER the action? The scene is suddenly filled with tension because we know there's a cat in the oven and we desperately want to find out what's going to happen!

Check the first paragraph of every stanza and see if there's a way to jump into the action sooner.

MURDER YOUR ADJECTIVES AND ADVERBS

Here's a quick grammar lesson. (It's the only one, I swear!)

Adjectives describe objects: red, green, round, tall, angry, crazy, perpendicular, odd, hairy, squirmy, etc.

Adverbs describe or modify actions: lazily, angrily, sleepily, adorably, quietly, ambiguously, carefully, forcibly, etc.

As a rule of thumb, you should rarely use more than one adjective to describe something, and if you can do without it, kill it!

At first, this sentence might seem acceptable:

The yellow sun was hidden behind white, fluffy clouds in the pale, blue, awe-inspiring sky.

There's nothing technically wrong with this, but let's remove the adjectives and consider the alternative:

The sun was hidden behind the clouds.

This sentence is shorter and easier to read, yet we don't seem to lose any description. *That's because we already know the sun is yellow.* Clouds are almost always white and fluffy, and they're always in the sky!

Here's the key: only use adjectives when something is out of the ordinary.

The sun appeared green as it shimmered through the canopy of leaves.

The sun isn't usually green, so this sentence is intriguing. What about adverbs?

Tristan tossed the ball perfectly into the basket.

"Yay!" the crowd cheered enthusiastically.

Again, "perfectly" and "enthusiastically" slow down the sentences and provide little information that's new. Since the ball made it into the basket, we know it was a close-to-perfect shot. When crowds cheer, it's almost always enthusiastically.

Like adjectives, adverbs are best used when they contradict the action.

The dog barked quietly.

The boy skipped lazily.

Both of these examples work because they add something new to the sentence while providing a more interesting picture in the reader's mind.

Search your writing for unnecessary adjectives and adverbs, and kill them!

A FEW MORE QUICK TIPS

The following tips weren't long enough for their own headings, but they're essential nonetheless!

Watch out for rhyming words and alliteration (a series of words that start with the same letter). Both will distract your readers and take them out of your story, so save them for poetry!

A single exclamation point goes a long way. You should always try to create the emphasis you need with the sentence itself, not punctuation. The best use of an exclamation point is in dialogue when people are shouting, otherwise, try to cut them! (Oops.)

Watch out for repetitive words, especially if they're unique. This is something you might not catch until a friend reads your work. I recently had a beta reader tell me I used the word "bestow" way too often. I searched my document... and they were absolutely right.

Dialogue tags are an important exception. You should stick with "he said" and "she said" ninety-percent of the time. "Yelled," "shouted," and "whispered," are acceptable in the appropriate situations, but attempts to be creative (hissed, groaned, chortled, etc.) can ruin the rhythm of your dialogue.

If you use chapter titles, make them intriguing! Don't spoil the book, but give the reader hints about the plot that make them want to reach each new chapter. This is especially effective if you have a table of contents at the beginning of your novel.

Watch out for the word "that." The general rule is simple: If your sentence makes sense without the word "that," get rid of it.

Walls of text are intimidating. Readers want to turn the page and see blank space. Space comes in the form of short paragraphs, rapid dialogue, stanza breaks, and chapter endings. Space allow the page—*and your readers*—to breathe. So if you have a solid page of description, break it up into paragraphs.

ADVANCED CONCEPTS

GROUND YOUR STORY IN REALITY

It doesn't matter if your story is about vampires who ride dragons, dragons who ride vampires, or alien life in the Andromeda Galaxy... you need to make your reader believe it.

In HBO's *The Wire* (arguably the closest TV has ever come to the novel format), the writers spend two and a half seasons building up the most realistic crime drama viewers have ever seen. The show's creator was an ex detective and used his experience to ensure every character and situation was as true-to-life as possible. In season three, a rogue cop devises a plan to legalize drugs in part of the city. As we experience every extreme facet of this make-believe experiment, *we believe every second*. This is only possible because the writers spent two years grounding us in reality.

If your story is about vampires who ride dragons, don't start chapter one with a vampire riding a dragon. Show us—in an engaging and succinct way—the day-to-day life of a vampire. Put them in a believable world with elements your readers (as mere humans) will understand. When reality has been established, introduce the dragons.

THE IMPORTANCE OF POINT OF VIEW

"Point of view" (or "POV") refers to the character the reader is following in the current scene. This will happen whether you're writing AS the character (*I went to the football game*) or ABOUT the character (*Maggie went to the football game*). Either way, you need to pick a single character to follow from the beginning of the scene until the end.

Which Character Do I Choose?

This won't be an issue if you're writing your book from a single character's point of view, but if you have multiple characters to choose from, here's a tip: *give the POV to the character who changes the most in the scene.* CHANGE is not only important, it's fun to read about! So if a character makes a big change in their life, make sure we're IN THEIR HEAD when it happens.

What Does it Mean to be in a Character's Head?

If you're writing from Gavin's point of view, the entire section will be about what GAVIN is thinking about. The reader will only hear birds chirping if Gavin hears birds chirping. The reader will only know what another character is thinking if they tell GAVIN what they're thinking.

What Should I Describe?

When you're writing from Gavin's POV, only show what grabs GAVIN'S attention. If he's in his bedroom, he probably wouldn't be looking at his bed unless something was out of the ordinary...

so if you want to describe his bed, *make it out of the ordinary.* Maybe his mom washed his white sheet with a red shirt and he just noticed it's slightly pink.

The same goes for descriptions of Gavin himself. He's not thinking about his hair unless he has a reason to think about his hair... so mess it up and THEN tell us about it.

Example

Look at this section from my book, *The Day I Wore Purple*:

Across the parking lot, through the revolving doors, down the familiar hospital corridor bustling with friends in white coats; Gavin rounded the corner to his brother's room and stopped short when he saw the prettiest girl he'd ever seen perched like a stone angel across from his usual spot. Orderlies and patients criss-crossed between them, but Gavin's eyes didn't leave the beauty sitting before him. (He suddenly became unshakably aware of the raptor on his shirt and wished to God he could go back in time to make a classier decision.)

He paused to let the adrenalin drain from his brain, then slowly and suavely sauntered to the bench across from the girl. He dropped his backpack on the linoleum and slouched.

The girl didn't notice him. Her attention was focused entirely on the painting in her lap where a neon Trapperkeeper served as a makeshift easel. She had yellow hair mixed with a little bit of red like the wispy part of a flame. Her shirt was white with tiny buttons, and the front was smeared with multi-colored fingerprints that reminded Gavin of a stained-glass window. He blamed the hospital for the sadness in her eyes.

The doctors and nurses are referred to as "friends" because this is how GAVIN sees them. We don't see what the girl is painting because GAVIN doesn't see it. We only know there's a raptor on his shirt because GAVIN is concerned about his appearance.

Following these rules will make your book easier to read and, more importantly, they'll help your readers identify with your characters.

THE @#$%! MOMENT

There's a moment in every work of fiction—novels, film, or television—where the protagonist's reality comes crashing down and a new problem presents itself.

Writing teachers call it the "inciting incident." I call it the #$%! moment.

The following rules are a general guide to crafting a kick-ass inciting incident. Must you follow them to write a good book? No. But I can promise you this: If you do it right, your readers will keep turning the page.

Example

The following text is a simplified list of scenes from *The Accidental Siren*. The #$%! moment is in italics.

-James and Whit make a movie in the woods.
-James is attacked by Danny and loses his precious camera.
-James returns home and lies to his family about the missing camera.
-James discovers an ad for a new camera.
-James goes to buy the camera and discovers a dozen boys in the trees around the home. They're in a trance, listening to the voice of a little girl inside.
-James meets the girl and they have dinner in a treehouse.
-The little girl is a modern-day siren... chaos ensues.

Make It Bad, Then Make It Worse

The goal of the #$%! moment is to hook your reader. You can't do this by beating around the bush or forcing your character to solve a mediocre problem. *You need to scare your protagonist and shock your audience.*

The #$%! moment needs to set up the central problem that will consume your characters for the rest of the book. Make it clear. Make it bad. Make it memorable.

In the above example, James could have simply heard the girl's voice. The scene would still be the inciting incident, but would it be exciting? No. To hook the reader, I added the boys in the trees. This puts a creepy image in the reader's mind and makes them wonder why the little girl is so special. Because we see the boys in a trance, we start to fear for James.

The Sooner The Better

If you place the inciting incident too late, the reader will get bored. If you place it too early, they won't understand it.

Here's the trick: *Let your protagonist determine the placement of the #$%! moment.* Are your characters average people like you and me? Or do we need to understand their complex lives in order to understand the inciting incident?

Before the #$%! moment, you need to establish what's normal.

In the example, I had three concepts to set up before the girl is introduced: James' family dynamic, his relationship to Whit, and his missing camera. The instant these story points are in place—*the instant the reader understands "normal"*—I hit them with the #$%! moment.

Plan Ahead

There's a reason I encourage writers to use a notecard system. If you plan your story before you write it, you can make sure that the inciting incident is as strong as possible. If you can't pinpoint the exact moment when "normal" comes crumbling down, you need to make it stronger!

And remember, the bigger the problem, the better the story.

ALWAYS PUSH THE STORY FORWARD

I'll say it a hundred times in this book: your primary goal is to make the reader turn the page. If they're not turning the page, you haven't done your job.

There are two methods guaranteed to keep your story moving.

The Ever-Changing Characters

We know from "The Importance of Point of View" that scenes should be shown from the perspective of the character who changes the most in that particular scene. Now let's take it a step further: If nobody changes in the scene, *the scene shouldn't exist.*

Look at the first scene in your book. Where is your character at the beginning of the scene? Where are they at the end? Did they learn anything? Did they make any important decisions? If not, either find a way to make them change... or cut the scene! (If you use a notecard system before you write, this will be much less painful.)

Tangoing with Obstacles

I like the word "tango" because it makes me imagine two people pushing and pulling each other back and forth across my story. To make it even sexier, the people are my protagonist and antagonist.

For every action your hero takes against your villain, *your villain needs to push back harder.* And when the villain pushes back, this spurs an *even stronger* response from your hero... which—you guessed it—prompts an *even crazier* response from the villain!

Again, a notecard system makes this easier. It's the best way to make sure this tango permeates every scene in your book. When I'm mapping out a new novel, I'll write my protagonist's name on twenty small cards and my antagonist's name on twenty more. Next, I tape one of the antagonist cards to the first action he takes against the hero (ideally the @#$%! moment!), then I go back and forth between hero and villain across the entire book. This helps me ensure that the conflict remains strong and that each scene becomes part of the tango.

The best writers won't stop with the villain... they'll map out a dance between the hero *and every obstacle the hero faces*. This can include internal conflicts, nature, family, Attention Deficit Disorder, zombies... anything and everything that keeps your protagonist from reaching their ultimate goal. The result is a tight, exciting plot that constantly propels the story forward.

DON'T SPELL THINGS OUT

Imagine assembling a jigsaw puzzle. Every time you find a piece that fits—every time you feel that delicious snap of cardboard and watch the colors line up—you feel a tiny rush of euphoria in the back of your brain. It's a minuscule feeling of course, but those tiny rushes build up every time you connect another new piece.

Your story should do the same thing in the mind of your reader.

There's a character in *The Wire* named Chris. Chris is muscle for a drug dealer, and we see his cold nature every time he kills. When Chris is sent to murder a child molester, his cool facade crumbles and he punches the man again and again until the man is unrecognizable.

I remember the moment that scene clicked for me; *Chris was probably molested as a child too*. The show never explicitly tells us this, so when I put the pieces together for myself, I got a tiny rush.

When done correctly, allowing readers to assemble the puzzle for themselves will make them active participants in your story. They'll have tiny "ah-ha!" moments, they'll feel pride for making subtle connections, and they'll read more closely to find other pieces of the puzzle.

This is a difficult line to walk (and one I'm still working on in my own work). You want to let the reader assemble the pieces themselves, but you NEED to make sure they understand important plot points. Hitting them over the head with a sledgehammer is better than leaving them confused! Since some readers may not put the pieces together as easily as others, it's best to implement this technique for character backstory or side plots.

Other books will talk at length about subtext (reading between the lines) and exposition (explaining backstory). If you learn to give your readers just enough information to put the pieces together themselves, you'll be on your way to mastering both of these complex tools!

THE KEY TO POWERFUL FLASHBACKS

Flashbacks can either be a tremendous asset to your story... or a tremendous burden on your reader. It's up to YOU to craft tight, informative scenes that depict your characters' backstory.

Be Brief

The biggest problem with flashbacks is that they remove the reader from the action. No matter how interesting they are, chances are the main story is more engaging.

Write Flashbacks "In the Moment"

Do you remember The Number One Rule? It applies to flashbacks too. Don't just TELL us about the flashbacks, SHOW us. Readers want dialogue and description *in the moment*, just like any other scene.

Inform the Present

The reader should gain new insight about the PRESENT during reflections on the PAST. If Kimmy is distraught over her father's death, try jumping back to the night of the fatal crash so we have more understanding of the pain Kimmy's experiencing in the present.

Juxtapose Mood

Another fun trick is to position happy flashbacks during tense scenes to underscore the pain of the current situation. If Mike and Justine are going through a divorce, this might be a good time to show us the first time they made love.

Create Suspense

By introducing a flashback after a cliffhanger, you can add tension to your scene. But remember the first rule of flashbacks: be brief! You can only push the suspense so far before readers get bored. And there's nothing worse for your story than a bored reader.

THERE'S NO SECRET TO GREAT DIALOGUE

I remember when my older brother watched a short film I made in college. The first thing he told me? "The dialogue sucks."

Being a persistent little writer, I plundered the shelves of Barnes & Noble for the perfect book about writing dialogue... and quickly discovered it doesn't exist.

Although I've never been able to find a quick fix for stale dialogue, I do have a few tricks that seem to improve banter between characters.

Fictional Dialogue is Not Real Dialogue

Some people have suggested you can learn to write dialogue by recording and studying real life conversations. DON'T DO THIS. Fictional dialogue is a dance. It has rhythm. It's heightened banter that you would never hear in real life. Nobody wants to read a book where characters talk like us. They don't want to be bogged down with the "ums" and "likes" and "uhs" that plague real-life conversation.

So how do you create engaging dialogue?

In the next few tips, I'm going to break up a full scene of dialogue from *The Accidental Siren* to illustrate each point.

Get In Late and Get Out Early

Readers don't want to hear hello and goodbye. They don't want to hear talk about the weather. They want the *meat*. They want THE GOOD STUFF. So start the conversation AFTER the pleasantries. Keep the reader active by making them play catch up with things the characters already know. Then end the dialogue before it gets stale.

This is the very beginning of a scene between James and Mara. No fluff. No small talk. Straight to the point.

> *"Why did you invite me here?" I asked. "Those things you said—"*
> *"I felt bad," Mara replied.*

(Continued below.)

Have Characters Interrupt Each Other

Interruptions are a good way to show a character's dominance, disrespect, or disinterest in a conversation. It can also create a staccato rhythm that will help pick up the pace.

> *"Why did you invite me here?" I asked. "Those things you said—"*
> *"I felt bad," Mara replied. "I wanted to tell you that I didn't mean it."*
> *"Then why—"*
> *She gave me the first cracker. "It's what Aunty wanted."*
> *I nibbled it. "Your aunty is weird. She sounded normal on the—"*
> *"She's not my real aunt."*

Don't Answer Questions Directly

Generic responses like "yes," "no," or "I don't know," are not only dull, but they're too definitive and can ruin the mystery of your scene. Instead, try answering questions with questions, answer them indirectly, or have the other character change the topic.

This can create tension that will keep readers hooked.

> "She's not *my real aunt*," Mara said.
> "Your grandma, then?"
> "Aunty is just what I call her."
> "Why? Who is she?"
> "We sleep in the same room." Mara nodded to the window, then popped a cheese-covered cracker in her mouth.
> "She's in there now? How'd you sneak out?"
> "Every Sunday she pulls out her wedding album and tells me the same stories over and over."
> "Stories?"
> "About her husband. He left."
> "Are the pictures all ripped up like the picture I saw in the frame?"
> "You're the first boy I've ever seen inside the house. Aunty hates them."

Silence Can Say More Than Words

Sometimes, not answering a question at all can speak volumes.

> "You're the first boy I've ever seen innside the house," Mara said. "Aunty hates them."
> "Them?" I asked.
> "Boys."
> "Do you hate boys too?"
> Mara dipped her finger in the cheese.

State the Obvious With Action, Not Dialogue

Instead of having a mother tell her son, "I love you," have her ruffle his hair and kiss him on the forehead. These are still clichés, but actions still speak louder than words.

> Mara dipped her finger in the cheese.
> A new ribbon of hair fell in a beautiful arc across her

brown eyes. I leaned forward, swept my fingers across her brow, and tucked the strands gently behind her ear.

Practice

The more you write, the more fluid your dialogue will become. But writing isn't the only way you can practice!

Read books with good dialogue. Better yet, attend stage plays. If you can't afford a night at the theater, rent movies or read scripts based on plays. *Glengarry Glen Ross, Who's Afraid of Virginia Woolf, Closer, Doubt*; these are all excellent plays made into films, and the dialogue is impeccable. Watch them over and over until the poetry of the words affects your own writing.

Not every exchange needs to sound like the bickering couples in *Closer* or the bantering college students in *The Social Network*, but your dialogue does need to engage your readers!

CREATE CHARACTERS,
NOT QUIRKS

I've spent years arguing with friends about the merits of movie director, Wes Anderson. The world loves him. I see his films as an adorable collection of quirks.

Margot Tenenbaum from *The Royal Tenenbaums* is the perfect example of "quirky." Margot was adopted. She's perpetually sullen. As a child, she directed elaborate stage plays about dead animals. She ran away from home to live in a museum. A stranger accidentally cut off her finger with an ax and now, as an adult, she sports a wooden finger on her right hand. She smokes. She wears dark eye liner. She once married a Jamaican recording artist. Her brother is falling in love with her. Etc, etc, etc...

What do these quirks add up to? The answer is not "character." Characters are created by THE DECISIONS THEY MAKE, not the clothes they wear or the weird things that happened in their past.

In order for quirks to work, they need to be LOADED. But how do you load a quirk?

Let's compare Margot's wooden finger to another infamous missing limb: Buster Bluth's lost hand in *Arrested Development*. In season two of my all-time-favorite comedy, Buster gets his hand bitten off by a loose seal.

The missing limb could have easily become a one-time gag. But in the hands of skillful writers, this "quirk" plays a pivotal role in Buster's life, the decisions he makes, the comedy of the show, and the plot as a whole. The missing hand emphasizes Buster's character traits, mainly *awkwardness*. There's endless wordplay such as the phrase "hand to God" and the doctor telling Buster's family he'll be "*all right*." There are brilliant moments of slapstick when Buster's stump is replaced with a hook in season two, then a massive prosthetic hand in season four. Buster's brother uses his missing limb as a life lesson for his kids, making it an integral part of the plot. There's foreshadowing before he loses the hand, metaphors tied to his lost hand, and SO MUCH MORE. The writers manage to squeeze every last drop of comedic and dramatic value out of this silly missing limb.

Now let's go back to *The Royal Tenenbaums*. Why was it important for Margot to lose a finger? The way she loses it is irrelevant to the story. It doesn't make her grow or change. It doesn't cause her to make different decisions that would give real insight into her character. It doesn't provide new insight into OTHER characters or storylines. And if it's a metaphor, it's over my head!

Consider this change. Little Margot Tenenbaum is a spunky child who loves her life and her adoptive family. She writes happy stage plays about LIVING animals and performs them for her friends. *But then it happens.* Margot's FATHER slips with an ax and lops off her finger! Her world turns upside down. She becomes detached. She writes plays about DEAD animals. She runs away from home. Her depression pushes her closer and closer to her brother who has fallen in love with her...

Now her wooden finger has meaning. When we see Margot tapping it against the side of the bathtub, we know exactly what she's thinking. It reminds us (and Margot!) that she used to be a fun-loving little girl. It builds tension between her and her father. And guess what? It's still quirky!

There's nothing wrong with quirks. Just make sure they serve a purpose.

EVIL DOESN'T EXIST

Without getting too metaphysical in this silly book, "evil doesn't exist" is one of the biggest life lessons I've learned from writing.

Villains—in fiction and in life—are not evil. The vast majority of humans on this planet *truly believe they're doing the right thing*. The few people who act evil for the sake of being evil are broken in ways they never asked for and cannot control.

Writing fiction requires you do delve into the heads of your antagonist, and when you do, you NEED to see their actions through THEIR eyes. What are their motivations? What happened in their past to make them want to hurt your protagonist? You don't need to love your bad guy, but you can't judge them either.

The Joker—Batman's ultimate nemesis—is the most infamous villain to break this rule. As far as we know, he really does just want to watch the world burn. But keep in mind the Joker represents a threat UNIQUE to Batman. Batman wants *order*... the Joker is *chaos*. Giving a backstory and motivations to this particular villain would actually make him less chaotic... and therefore, a weaker opponent to Batman.

The vast majority of villains won't share this dynamic with the protagonist, so chaos won't cut it. They need to have sympathetic backstories, believable motivations for their actions, and absolute conviction that they're doing the right thing.

The reader doesn't always need to empathize with your villain, *but you do.*

EVERYONE NEEDS A
THROUGH-LINE

If you write detailed characters in the beginning of your book, make sure you don't abandon them in later chapters. Minor characters should serve a clear purpose in the life of your protagonist. If they don't have any affect on your main character, then they probably shouldn't be in your story. Every major character should contribute to the climax in some way. They don't have to be present in the last scene, but their influence should be felt by both the protagonist and the reader.

This tip applies to objects too. Have you heard the phrase, "If you show a gun in act one, it better go off in act three"?

The SECOND use of a loaded object can create a legitimate surprise since readers have been trained to expect a single payoff. If you've watched every season of *Game of Thrones*, you'll remember Tyrian and the viewer learn about wildfire in the beginning of season two. The mysterious weapon is finally put to use at the end of the season during the Battle of Blackwater which provides a spectacular payoff. Then, George RR Martin lets us forget about wildfire for several seasons (several YEARS if you watched the show as it aired)... then brings it back again in an even bigger way.

Here's a great trick if you're stuck on a later chapter. Think about all the bit players or important objects sprinkled through your story. Is there a way to bring them back with a renewed purpose, as if all their previous interactions with the protagonist were culminating into this one moment? If you use this trick, make sure you rewrite earlier scenes to foreshadow their epic return!

MAKE EVERY ENDING COUNT

And by "every ending," I mean EVERY ENDING. The end of your book, the end of your chapter, *the end of your sentence.*

Again, making your reader turn the page is the only thing that matters. Unfortunately, every ending—large and small—gives them an opportunity to stop. To make sure they don't, you need to make your endings count.

Ending Sentences

Here are two versions of the same paragraph from my book, *Fallout Dreams:*

As Nolan pillaged the shelf for something to save him, he had the sudden realization that a bear really had *mauled Gary. It was a grizzly son of a bitch, buried in its den, storing up food, just waiting for spring. Now it was waking up.*

Look at the first and third sentences. Both of them are technically correct, and neither of them sound particularly awkward. But lets change around a few words and see if we can make them more powerful.

As Nolan pillaged the shelf for something to save him, he had the sudden realization that Gary really was *mauled by a bear. It was a grizzly son of a bitch, buried in its den, storing up food, just waiting for spring. Now it was awake.*

"Bear" and "awake" are stronger words than "Gary" and "up."

This may seem like a minor detail, but powerful sentences build on each other over time creating a rhythm to your writing that will keep your reader focused until the end of the chapter.

Ending Chapters

Most people rarely finish a book in one sitting, and when they take a break, it's usually between chapters.

Your goal is to make the ending of your chapter HAUNT your reader until don't have a choice but to see what happens next.

When structuring your book, make sure every chapter builds to its own mini climax and culminates with either a madness-inducing question, a terrible revelation, a raising of the stakes, or a cliffhanger.

This applies to stanzas as well, though stanza breaks shouldn't end as dramatically as chapter breaks.

Ending Books

Your sentences kept readers hooked to the end of the chapters. Your chapters kept them enthralled until the end of the book... but did your ending make them want to read your next story?

The best book endings will live in a reader's mind until the day they die. The next section gives important pointers for writing a spectacular climax.

ESSENTIAL TRICKS FOR
A SPECTACULAR CLIMAX

I try to be honest with myself regarding my talent. I'm bad at exposition, my books are too long, and I still can't spell "restaurant" without spellcheck. I do, however, take pride in my endings... and love sharing my methodology with other writers!

Endings are important to me because they keep me motivated to finish my books. I see what's coming. I get excited. I plow forward. You want your readers to do the same.

A good climax takes careful planning and an exquisite understanding of your plot and characters, but when it's done right, it's *gorgeous*.

The Perfect Climax is Simple and Swift

You've had a dozen chapters to immerse your readers fully in the world of your creation. By the time the climax begins, we should know your characters inside and out. We know what they look like. We know what they're thinking. We know their motivations *better than they do*.

We know what they want and what they need to do in order to get it.

There should be virtually no exposition at the end of your book; no fancy descriptions, no internal monologues. Everything that had to be explained should have been explained in earlier chapters *because that's what earlier chapters are for*. The first 9/10ths of your story needs to plant the seeds that will finally bloom—rapidly and cohesively—in these last few pages.

With everything else stripped away, only DIALOGUE and ACTION will remain to propel us to your gripping conclusion.

The Perfect Climax Will Implement Character Strengths

In Hitchcock's *Rear Window,* Jefferies is a photographer stuck in a wheelchair. Unable to move, he uses the zoom lens on his camera to catch a murderer in the apartments across the street. When the murderer discovers Jefferies and breaks into his home, our handicapped hero uses the flash on his camera to blind him until help arrives.

Jefferies' camera (aka *profession*) saves his life not once, but twice. This makes his occupation seem like an integral part of the story, and when it pays off in the climax, it brings an elegant cohesion to the story.

The Perfect Climax Will Mirror the @#$%! Moment

In *Eternal Sunshine of the Spotless Mind,* the @#$%! moment occurs when Joel agrees to a radical medical procedure that deletes his memories of Clementine, the woman who broke his heart. In the end, Joel and Clementine receive strange cassette tapes from the company that erased their brains. They play the tapes at the same time and are shocked to hear themselves talking about all the reasons they hated each other. While still listening to the incriminating tapes, Joel and Clementine decide to move past their failed relationship to try it all again.

The tapes tie the climax directly to the @#$%! moment. In fact, the tapes were recorded DURING the @#$%! bringing even more symmetry to this lovely finale.

The Perfect Climax Will Dictate Your Theme

Apocalypse Now is one of my all-time favorite movies. A man named Willard is sent into the jungle to kill Kurtz, a rogue solider who descended into madness after years at war. The climax of the movie shows Willard covered in war paint, slashing Kurtz to death, and emerging from the experience as a bloodied solider haunted by the same madness as his victim.

What is the theme of *Apocalypse Now*? Madness. Digging deeper, it's about how madness is contagious. It's about *the heart of darkness*. This theme permeates every scene of the film before culminating with the image of a changed man stained in the blood of his enemy.

It's okay if you've been writing your book without much consideration of theme. Instead of imposing a theme on your story before you know what it's really about, wait until your climax is set in stone, analyze the decisions your characters make to determine your theme, then go back through your book to strengthen this theme through dialogue, character, and visual motifs.

The Perfect Climax Isn't Resolved

Yes, readers need resolution. Ending your story without questions answered or lessons learned is a bad idea. However, you don't have to answer EVERY question. If you leave some aspects of your conclusion open-ended, your readers will be thinking about your book long after they turn the final page.

At the end of *Social Network*, Mark Zuckerberg sits at his laptop in an empty law firm hitting refresh after sending his girlfriend a friend request on Facebook. The movie ends without showing us if the girl ever accepted, and that's okay! On a larger scale, we wonder about Zuckerberg's very soul. Did he learn anything from the lawsuits that put him in this position? Will he ever learn to treat people with the respect they deserve? The filmmakers never give concrete answers to these questions. The result is a happy(ish) ending that leaves viewers with a lingering curiosity that will follow them out of the theater.

The Perfect Climax Is UNEXPECTED and INEVITABLE

The reader should reach the end of your story and think to themselves, "I didn't see this coming... but it couldn't end any other way!"

Instead of providing another example, I want you to recall your favorite climax to a book or film. Do you remember the first time you experienced it? Were you surprised by the way it ended? Could it have ended any other way?

If you've seen the films mentioned above, you'll know that all of them follow all of these rules exquisitely: they're fast-paced; the main characters use strengths that were established earlier in the stories; the events that put each story in motion are mirrored in the events that finish them; the themes are woven magically into the way characters ultimately deal with their problems; the endings ask more questions than they answer; and none of the stories could have ended any other way, yet we never see the endings coming.

DEVELOPING USEFUL HABITS

DESTROY YOUR FAVORITE NOTEBOOK

Do you have a favorite brand of pen that draws *that perfect line*? Do you meticulously clean your desk before you start writing? Is there a certain time of the day that you MUST write or you can't focus? If the answer is yes to any of these questions, it's time to shake up your habits!

Writers need to be spontaneous. We never know when or where inspiration will strike. Maybe we have the perfect routine, but how do we know that routine will last? We can't shut off our imaginations because we're on vacation, transitioning to a new job, or dealing with life's countless problems.

The fact is, our well-meaning habits can become an excuse for procrastination.

Do you find yourself falling into this trap? Try writing outside your routine. Force yourself to work in a chaotic environment. Don't get locked into a favorite desk, candle scent, time of day, or notebook.

I had the idea for this tip while I was on vacation with family. I was on a boat surrounded by six kids, four adults, and a dog. My hands were wet. I was sunburnt. All I had was an old receipt and a pen. But I still managed to write a page of notes for my next book.

Bottom line: never let your tools stifle your inspiration!

TEXT LIKE YOU WRITE

I've had dozens of hopeful writers email me, *"y dont ppl take me serious when i say im a writter?"*

I don't need to point out the irony.

When you text, email, blog, or tweet, *use the opportunity to hone your skills.*

Use email correspondences to enhance your vocabulary. Use Twitter to perfect your pithy anecdotes. Use texts to practice economy. Use message boards to test the most powerful ways to structure a sentence.

Honing your skills is enough of a reason to change your daily habits, but there's an even more important reason: *You need to look professional.*

Lawyers need to wear suits and ties to assure clients their *own* life is in order. Therapists need to refrain from gossiping. Photographers need to scrutinize their Instagram pictures before posting. But writers are lucky! We can wear whatever we want. We can refuse to shave. We can talk to ourselves on the subway or ask random people odd questions. We can get away with these things because they're expected of us. But there's one major exception: *writers need to write well.*

If you want to be a professional writer, then present yourself as a professional writer.

LEARN FROM TV

Bookworms often look down on TV shows for their mind-numbing plots, easy laughs, and art-destroying politics. But if this is your only perception of TV, you're missing a fantastic learning opportunity.

Here are a few ways you can turn your TV into a writing workshop.

Don't Watch Crap

This includes game shows, episodic police dramas, most sitcoms, and the Kardashians. Yes, reality shows have writers... but I'll save that rant for another time.

Search the internet for TV Top Ten lists. Find programs that are known for their outstanding writing. And don't be afraid to watch shows that are off the air! The most inspiring TV comes from the Golden Age of HBO.

For drama, I would recommend *The Wire*, *The Shield*, *Deadwood*, *Breaking Bad*, *Six Feet Under*, *Game of Thrones*, *Fargo*, *House of Cards*, *The Leftovers*, and the first three seasons of *Lost*. For Comedy, try *Arrested Development*, *Community*, *Entourage*, *Summer Heights High*, *Malcolm in the Middle*, *30 Rock*, *Rick and Morty*, *Bojack Horseman*, and the first two seasons of *The Office*.

Be Involved

Yes, you can enjoy a show just as you would enjoy a good book, but never let your brain go to sleep! Always ask yourself: "Why did the writers do that?" "What influenced these decisions?" "How could the ending be better?" "How do these episodes fit together in the context of the season?" "Why was that funny?" "Why did that make me cry?" "Why DIDN'T that make me cry?"

Watch for character arcs. Study them. Pay attention to how characters interact. Are there any story lines that the writers plant in season one that pay off in season five? The best shows will do that. Do you notice any patterns from show to show? Do any of these patterns relate to novels? Is the show episodic? Or do you need to see the prior episodes to understand the plot? What seasons seem to lag? Why? Hug your notebook through the whole show and take notes when you discover a clever writing device.

Discuss

I have several friends who love good TV as much as I do. After we watch an episode, we dissect it. We get excited about what works. We get disappointed about what doesn't. We rant about the last three seasons of *Lost*. We quote favorite lines of dialogue. We argue.

Find a friend who shares your tastes. Pop a bowl of popcorn, have a *Breaking Bad* marathon, and start a dialogue about the intricacies of the fabulous writing.

Dig Deeper

Head over to YouTube after you finish a show. There are hundreds of channels dedicated to dissecting every aspect of TV and movies from characters to themes to philosophy. This is an excellent and fun way to expand your understanding of the craft.

PSYCHOLOGY, PHILOSOPHY, THEOLOGY, HISTORY, SCIENCE, AND MORE

Every writer has a specialized knowledge outside of writing. Some of us know about animal training, skateboarding, corporate finance, food preparation, hotel management, astronomy, or pop culture. Whether you do it on purpose or not, your unique insights will worm their way into your writing... and they should! People like to read the details and secrets of unfamiliar professions and your insider knowledge will bring authenticity to your work. (More on this later.)

There are, however, important types of knowledge that could be necessary to your story. Are you writing a science-fiction novel? You probably need to understand the basics of science. Psychological thriller? Historical drama? Existential comedy? Even if these aren't your usual genres, "big concepts" can pop up in any work of fiction and you need to be prepared.

Dedicate a bookshelf to introductory reference books, beginner's guides, "For Dummies" books... there are entire series dedicated to teaching the basics of vast or difficult concepts. Search them out, page through them when you're bored, and keep them close while you write.

Not only are these resources useful for understanding big concepts, but they can be a great source of inspiration.

This goes without saying, but I'll say it anyway. If you're writing about a specific concept such as manic depressive disorder, the origin of Hinduism, or a vaccine that will end aging, you need to research these topics thoroughly. Michael Crichton didn't write *Jurassic Park* by reading *Chaos Theory For Dummies*.

In short, be an expert at a few things, but understand the basics of everything.

FOUR SOLUTIONS TO WRITER'S BLOCK

We've all read countless blog posts about how to cure writer's block. But did they work? What if you don't have the luxury to "set your book aside for a few weeks" or the patience to fill out a list of writing prompts?

As with all of these tips, the following suggestions come from personal experience. It's been seven years since I discovered these tricks, and I haven't had writer's block since.

Use a Notecard System

Stephen King doesn't do this. Stephen King jots an idea on a sheet of paper, then develops the story as he goes.

Stephen King is a genius.

For the rest of us, his method can be dangerous. Writer's block will thrive when we don't know where the story is going. So what can you do differently? Plan your story before you write it.

Before I begin a new book, I plot my story on giant notecards and arrange them on the wall in chronological order. Every time I have a new idea for a scene, I write it on a small card and tape it to the large one. When I have a rough idea of where the story is going, I finally begin to write. I pull off the first card, read the notes, and incorporate them into the scene. When I get to the next scene, I know exactly what needs to happen.

Never Use Writer's Block As an Excuse To Procrastinate

If you blame writer's block for your lack of progress, this will only give your brain a reason to shut down more frequently. Instead of playing video games until inspiration strikes, train yourself to work no matter what.

This doesn't mean you can't step away from the computer. Work on your notecards. Ponder future scenes, and figure out where your current scene fits in. Do jumping jacks while you study your notes to increase your serotonin levels! Whatever you do, don't let your mind think it's acceptable to quit.

Read a Favorite Book

This seems to go against what I just said about not taking breaks, but stick with me.

Before you delve into a beloved passage, grab your notebook and pen. Open your mind. As you read, filter every word through thoughts of your own project. Let the characters, structure, and style influence you. Sometimes you'll stumble on a passage that works but you don't know why. Reread it. Then read it again. When an idea strikes, write it down.

The key is to read a book that you already know inside and out. If you start a new story, you risk closing your mind to your own work as you get sucked into an exciting plot.

Get Out of Your Comfort Zone

Shake up your routine! Surround yourself with people. Use a new pen. Write outside. Listen to loud music. Grab a bagel at Panera. Whatever you do, force your brain to work outside its usual habits. Sometimes routine is good. Sometimes breaking routine is better.

THERE'S NO EXCUSE NOT TO LEARN

This little book is only the beginning.

Here's a quick list of how-to books that have inspired me over the last several years. I hope they help you on your journey as a writer!

Writing a Great Movie - Jeff Kitchen
I learned more from this book than the rest combined. Yes, it's for screenwriters, but novelists NEED TO KNOW this stuff, and often overlook it. It covers structure, characters, and most importantly, DRAMA. (I summarize Kitchen's advice in the next chapter.)

On Writing - Stephen King
The master weaves his writing tips into a personal memoir. Not only helpful, but inspirational.

Writing Tools: 50 Essential Strategies for Every Writer - Roy Peter Clark
When I began my first novel, I hadn't written prose since high school. This book is filled with practical tips for novelists and journalists.

Story - Robert McKee
I never read the book itself, but I listened to the audiobook four times. Some criticize Robert McKee for being too formulaic or mainstream. Those people rarely have writing careers.

It Was the Best of Sentences, It Was the Worst of Sentences - June Casagrande
This is one of those annoying books that you don't want to read but know you should. Ms. Casagrande makes grammar rules simple and practical. I strongly recommend this book to anyway who wants to take their writing to the next level.

There is no excuse not to learn! If you can't afford books on writing, watch YouTube. There are thousands of channels dedicated to writing tips from amateurs and pros alike. Better yet, search out interviews with your favorite writers, and don't forget to jot down notes if inspiration strikes!

TAKE CRITICISM SERIOUSLY, BUT NOT TOO SERIOUSLY

When someone offers me advice on my work, I only consider it for one of two reasons:

They convince me completely.

Other readers are saying the same thing.

If my best friend reads my work and strongly suggests that I remove my very favorite ending, I'll thank him for his advice, but I probably won't make the change. If my girlfriend reads my novel and tells me I need to change my brilliant ending, I still won't change it. If my mom and my professor and my cousin have *the exact same critique...* then it's time for me to admit that I did something wrong.

Not everybody is going to love everything about your book. If you start changing things to fit what people want, you'll lose your voice. However, you can't afford to stay hard-headed if the same advice is coming from multiple readers. If it is, you need to open yourself to making difficult changes.

Chances are that—in the end—you'll realize your readers were right.

WHAT READERS WANT

DRAMA

So your writing is incredible, your descriptions are sexy, your characters are funny, and you have a concept that'll impress Suzanne Collins herself. But is there DRAMA in your story? Or is it just... story?

Drama keeps readers hooked to the page. Drama takes a series of events and turns them into emotional scenes. Drama raises questions in the readers mind; questions they want answered NOW. Drama is the surest way to put the reader in the character's shoes.

There are three tricks I use to introduce drama into my story:

Take Advantage of Point of View

If you're writing from third-person POV, you'll have many opportunities to add drama.

Try this: Use a different character's POV to give the reader information that your main character doesn't have. Maybe Keaton (and the reader) learns that Mike's wife is cheating on him. When we cut back to a banal conversation between Mike and his wife, their simple dialogue has been enriched with drama because we know what Mike's wife is thinking about... and he doesn't. This scene can have the worst dialogue in the world and the reader will still be scrutinizing every line for meaning.

Force a Dilemma On Your Protagonist

(I'll try to discuss this concept without ranting about *The Hunger*

Games.)

A dilemma occurs when a person is faced with two choices with equal stakes. Should I go to college or take the high-paying job? Should I tell my friend his wife is cheating on him, or should I keep it a secret? Should I let the Nazis take my son... or my daughter?

Characters NEED to make decisions. It's the writer's job to present them with two of their greatest fears and force them to pick one. You need to put the reader inside the protagonist's brain as he tries to determine the best path to success. And whatever you do, don't pull a "Katniss and Peeta both live" and break the impending conflict. *Make Katniss choose.* If you don't, you could lose your reader.

This is not just about building drama, it's about building *character*. The biggest indication of CHARACTER is the decisions one makes under pressure. And dilemma is the best way to build that pressure.

Build Expectations... Then Destroy Them

Jason has been called to the principal's office twelve times before today. It's the same lecture every time... the same slap on the wrist before getting sent back to class as if nothing happened.

Now, Jason treads down the hall toward the stupid principal's office. He opens the office door. Standing beside the principal are his parents, teachers, and two of his best friends, all glaring at him with their arms crossed.

By telling the reader about Jason's past experiences in the principal's office, we've created expectations in their minds about what's going to happen next. When Jason sees his loved ones standing with the principal, expectations have been destroyed and the reader experiences a visceral reaction. This is another form of drama.

Keep in mind that this example is TELLING the reader what to expect. Imagine the impact if we actually SHOWED Jason's previous interactions with the principal, then waited until the third time to include the parents and friends.

Creating dilemma and expectations can be used for GOOD too. Someone could be forced to choose between two awesome outcomes... and the drama remains. Maybe Jason's parents get called to the principal's office every time Jason gets in trouble... but this time, the principal pats him on the back and tells him he made the honor roll. Either way, the reader's emotions will be heightened if their expectations are destroyed.

Sacrifice Surprise For Suspense

Hitchcock gave the classic example of two men having a mundane conversation in a diner. They talk and talk and talk... then *KA-BOOM!* A bomb explodes beneath the table, the men are killed, and the audience is surprised.

Surprise can be fun, but it's a momentary experience. Suspense, on the other hand, can last for hours. Consider this: what if we show a ticking time bomb beneath the table *before* the men sit down? The reader will be on the edge of their seat for the whole conversation.

This technique is a great way to spice up boring exposition while adding a dose of drama to your story.

DISCOVERY

When we're children, our lives are filled with discovery. Everywhere we turn we see something marvelous we've literally never seen before. Discovery becomes less frequent as we grow older, but our inquisitive nature and adventurous spirit never dies. Some adults turn to travel to find new experiences. Some turn to drugs. Most turn to stories.

That's where you come in.

Have you mastered the art of showing rather than telling? Have you grounded your story in reality? Have you established a solid point of view? Then giving your reader a sense of discovery will be easy.

Experience Discovery Through Character

When Brennan stumbles into the witch's basement, *show us his reaction*. Don't TELL us he's scared, but give him verbs that indicate how he's feeling about the discovery. He doesn't walk toward the crimson candle still burning on an old cinderblock, *he inches toward it*. He doesn't feel his heartbeat, *he hears the blood pulsing against the inside of his ear*.

Also, what are his thoughts regarding the creepy basement? Does it remind him of a past experience? Does it unearth something carnal inside him? Delve into the mind of Brennan and allow him to expound on the personal significance of his discovery.

Experience Discovery Through Description

Moments of discovery should contain the best descriptions in your book. Interesting explorations are one of the few times when long descriptions won't bore your readers, so feel free to uncover every detail, describing each new discovery as if you're unearthing a dinosaur skeleton one bone at a time. (Don't forget to put the cat in the oven first to keep your readers engaged!)

Examples From Fiction

In *2001: A Space Odyssey,* Arthur C. Clarke goes into painstaking detail about an astronaut's experience as he travels to the moons of Saturn, transcends space and time, and learns about the origin of his species.

In *Jurassic Park,* Crichton puts us in the heads of dinosaur-loving archeologists before sending them into an underground raptor nest. Because we feel connected to the characters—because the details of the nest are vital to their survival—our interest is held for a dozen pages and our thirst for discovery is quenched.

In *The Inferno,* Dante is led through the depths of hell while describing each new layer in mortifying detail. The hook of the entire story is a simple question: *what new horrors will Dante discover next?*

The discovery doesn't have to be as massive as space or dinosaurs or hell. In *The Virgin Suicides,* a group of boys learn about the girls next door through a telescope, the girls' trash, and third-person accounts. Like the boys, the reader hangs on every minuscule discovery in hopes of learning more about the mysterious girls.

DARKNESS

I read an interview with Stephen King where he had this to say about a book he just read: *"In short, there was nothing there to disturb the soul in the slightest."*

I wrote down the quote and taped it to my desk. But why?

Believe it or not, humans want to experience darkness. We're drawn to it. We're endowed with morbid curiosity. We slow down at car crashes. We lean forward when friends gossip about another friend's divorce. We subject ourselves to 24/7 news coverage bombarding us with ten stories about hate for every one about love *because advertisers know fear sells*. We spend a hundred dollars for a single day at a theme park where we're thrust into the sky and flipped upside down at breakneck speed. We flock to horror movies—even if they're awful—*just to feel scared*. We visit museums dedicated to humanity's greatest horrors such as such as The Holocaust Memorial Museum.

Obviously, nobody ACTUALLY wants to get in a car crash. Nobody wants to experience divorce, flail helplessly through the air, come face-to-face with a horror-show villain, or experience the tragedy of the holocaust. But we do want to experience these things from a distance.

As Dante's *Inferno* demonstrates, BOOKS are the safest way to visit hell.

It's the fiction writer's job to satisfy the darkest desires of their readers. Put your protagonist in the worst possible situation given the parameters of your story. Push them to a place where reasonable people are too afraid to tread. Force them into dilemmas that would make a grownup sob. Find a way to ruin their lives... then make things worse. *And show us the ramifications.*

Here's the most important part: when you amp up the darkness, *the light will shine brighter than ever.*

HBO's *Deadwood* is made up of the most vulgar characters on television. They beat prostitutes, toss around racial slurs, fart, stab each other in the backs (literally and figuratively), drink too much, plot against their country, feed their enemies to pigs, and brawl in piss and mud. But when the foul-mouthed Jane and her filthy partner sing an off-key rendition of *Row Row Row Your Boat* to a sick little girl, the beauty of the moment sends chills down the viewer's limbs. If the characters spent the whole show singing pretty songs to sick kids, the moment would be sappy instead of beautiful.

Not every book needs to be a horror story, but playing it safe doesn't hold the reader's attention. Even in happy novels, I would recommend at least one scene that takes the readers into an experience darker than they were expecting. Make it surreal. Make it uncomfortable. Give them a sense of PERSPECTIVE so they truly appreciate the joy in the rest of the story.

In this age of trigger warnings and safe spaces, it's the writer's duty to rape the imagination... to lure readers with an engaging story before destroying them with their greatest fears. This isn't cruel. *It's teaching them to see beauty in the profane.* If you have a hopeful ending, you can rebuild your readers piece by piece until they emerge stronger than they were when they first picked up your book.

CATHARSIS

At the time of this writing, I've been married and divorced three times. The first two relationships were hard on me (to put it mildly), but the third was good. When #3 left me for another guy, I fell into a deep depression and—for the first time in my life— searched out professional help. I'll never forget the first thing my therapist told me. *He said it was okay to feel sad.* I wasn't just ALLOWED to feel angry, I was ENCOURAGED to feel angry. It seemed backwards at the time, but he told me that EXPERIENCING pain was the first step toward ESCAPING it.

So I did. I cried when I was sad. I listened to loud music when I was pissed. I empathized with heartbroken songwriters. I watched movies about people going through similar experiences and I sobbed alongside them.

And it helped. It was *cathartic.*

Healthy people long to release their pent-up emotions. We want to be frightened. We want to be moved to tears. We want to see others fighting the same battles we've been fighting for years. This is how we exorcise our demons.

How Can a Writer Help?

Many of the steps toward creating a cathartic experience have already been covered in the sections *"Ground Your Story In Reality," "The @#$%! Moment," "Essential Tricks for a Spectacular Climax," "Drama,"* and the last segment on darkness. But there are more.

Find What Your Character Wants... And Withhold It

If Troy wants his sick girlfriend to get better... *make the girlfriend sicker.*

Sustain this tension for as long as your reader can bear it. Give Troy hope, then bring him to the point of snapping. Make your reader WANT to throw your book away... but engage them just enough so they won't. When you've reached the breaking point of both Troy and the reader, THIS is when you have the power to grant catharsis.

But how do you do it?

Either let his girlfriend live... or let her die.

More broadly, let your protagonist achieve their ultimate goal... or lose it forever.

Examples from Cinema

When the wrongfully-accused prisoner stands with his arms open in the lightning and rain at the end of *The Shawshank Redemption*; when the plane barrels toward the Earth in *United 93*; when the dysfunctional family dances together on stage in *Little Miss Sunshine*; when the young drummer defies his teacher and gives the performance of a lifetime in *Whiplash*; when a sympathetic Nazi realizes his pen could have saved two more lives in *Schindler's List*; when a repressed husband recognizes the beauty in his life the second before he dies in *American Beauty*... these are the moments that grab hold of our stomachs and our brains and our hearts. These are the moments that make us cheer... or cry... *or both.*

And that is catharsis.

TRUTH

Writers are always preaching about "truth" in writing.

Until recently, this has been an abstract concept for me. I know what it means to "tell the truth," but how does this relate to my story? Isn't fiction a lie by definition?

Digging For TRUTH

First, you need to dig toward the REALISTIC core of your story. When you find it, expose it to the world through character and plot.

Since I have intimate knowledge of my own work and process, I'll use *The Accidental Siren* again as an example.

Siren is a story about a twelve-year-old girl named Mara Lynn. Mara is objectively the most beautiful person in the world. James Parker is also twelve. He, like the rest of the world, has a strong, unnatural attraction to Mara. The idea for this story began as a simple "what if" concept: "What if there was a girl more beautiful than anyone in the world?"

If we stand on the surface of this idea, we might write a generic paranormal romance about a boy who's obsessed with a girl. But if we pursue TRUTH, we'll find ourselves digging to the very essence of this concept. We can find the truth by asking ourselves, "What would ACTUALLY happen if a prepubescent boy met the prettiest girl alive?"

He would:
-like her.
-love her.
-dream about her.
-try to keep her for himself.
-objectify her.
-feel bad for objectifying her.
-*hate himself* for objectifying her.
-lie for her.
-fight for her.
-kill for her?
-hit puberty sooner.
-ask friends about sex.
-read books about sex.
-experiment with his own sexuality.
-attempt to be different from other boys.
-find ways to prove he's different from other boys.
-betray his friends for her affection.
-betray his family for her affection.
-betray himself for her affection.
-see her as unique.
-see her as supernatural.
-see her as God.

Hopefully this list helps clarify what I mean by "digging." If we stop after the first few layers, we are not telling the truth, but rehashing clichés.

Notice that the goal of this exercise was NOT to be provocative. I wasn't looking to offend readers with my book. I just followed the truth as far as a 30-something male from Michigan could. I drew from my past experiences as a twelve-year-old. Like most guys, I remember the experience. *Unlike* most guys, I'm willing to be honest about it.

Now that we know how to dig for truth using "What if" questions, how do we identify the truth when it's uncovered?

First, lets look at the qualities of truth.

Truth is Universal

It doesn't matter if your story is a romance between a flying turtle and a jelly bean. If you tell your story with honesty, everyone will be able to identify with it.

Truth is Unique

You may be searching in familiar territory (love, death, hope, obsession, terror), but when you discover truth, it will be something special... something *only you* could find.

Truth is Provocative

If you reach a question that makes you think, "Whoa... I don't know if I should go there..." chances are you're on the right track.

Truth is Captivating

Because it's universal, unique, and provocative, people are captivated by honesty.

Examples

"Death is sad," is not truth. It's an observation that is often true, but not always.

What happens if you're Nate Fisher from the third season of *Six Feet Under*? Here's a man who threw his life away by marrying a woman he knocked up. He hates the banality of his new life. He might even hate his wife.

But then she goes missing. Several episodes go by and nobody can find her. Death is the only explanation.

"Sad" doesn't begin to describing Nate's emotions. Neither does "relief." Nate (and the *Six Feet Under* writers) had to dig deeper to find truth. Through his wife's death, *Nate discovers that he actually loved her*. He feels *guilty* for wishing her out of his life. He misses her *despite his newfound freedom*. Truth, in this instance, is a horrific crucible of emotions that never would have been unearthed if the writers had stopped at "sad."

If I was writing a scene about death before my father died, I WOULD have stopped at "sad." I wouldn't have been able to write about how my nightmares became comforting because my reality was worse. I wouldn't have known about the hatred I'd feel towards doctors for limiting a patient's morphine intake. I didn't know the worst part about my father's death would be the fact that he'd never see me succeed as a writer.

Now scan this tip again. I bet you were mildly interested in the first half... but I bet you were fully immersed in the last two paragraphs.

THAT'S the power of truth.

DIFFICULT TRUTHS FOR SERIOUS WRITERS

(A NOTE BEFORE YOU CONTINUE)

If writing is your hobby, stop reading now.

If you're just beginning your journey as a writer, set this chapter aside, fall in love with books, revel in the process, develop your voice, share your stories with people you love, and come back later.

If writing is your dream career, forge ahead.

DON'T WRITE WHAT YOU KNOW

For two years I worked as a reader at a tiny Los Angeles production company. Every day my boss would hand me another screenplay to read, summarize, and review. In four out of five of these screenplays, the writer took the advice of every teacher from elementary school to college... *they wrote what they knew.*

It turns out most people don't know much.

Nobody wants to read about your life. They don't want hear about your on-again-off-again relationships, the weight you've been gaining, or—worst of all—your struggles as a writer.

When it comes to writing fiction, your teachers were wrong.

Luckily, there are successful authors out there who came up with much better advice:

Don't Write What You Know... Write What You WANT To Know

George RR Martin has never ruled over a continent, beheaded peasants, or planned for war. He did, however, grow up with an intense fascination of European history. He had centuries of kings and queens and battles and medieval politics to draw from before he ever touched *Game of Thrones*. And when he needed more insight, I bet he enjoyed the research!

Write About Experiences You WANT to Know... And People You DO Know

This is my own variation of the tip. I research and imagine out-of-this-world EXPERIENCES, but I look inward when I write my CHARACTERS.

In *Hitchhiker's Guide To the Galaxy*, Douglas Adams tells a fantastic tale of spaceships and aliens and impossible planets he will never experience in a thousand lifetimes. However, his main character is a lonely Brit who likes to visit the pub after work. This lets Adams delve honestly and easily into the mind of his central character which grounds the crazy story in reality.

Writing about a character similar to yourself allows you to spice up your story with your own unique perspective. You can finally release your inner monologues, pet peeves, and theories about the meaning of life. And this can be a great source of originality! But when it comes to big picture ideas, expand your horizons to the end of the universe.

PUT STORY BEFORE CAUSE

Some might call me a bigot for discussing this rule, but it needs to be said.

Nobody cares that you're gay. Nobody cares that you're black or brown or disabled or morbidly obese. Nobody cares that you're a feminist or a buddhist or a proud democrat. Nobody cares that your dad died in a car accident or that your mom has cancer.

But tell a good story and they'll read it.

Some people write novels to promote a cause. This is fantastic if you're writing non-fiction, but prioritizing CAUSE before STORY can destroy a work of fiction.

Christians read Christian books. The rest of the world laughs at them, not because they're about Christian values, but because they're usually bad. The writer's goal was not to captivate and entertain his readers but to promote a message. Not only does this make for a bad story, it limits the book's potential audience and the writer ends up preaching to the choir.

Having said that, it is VITAL to follow the earlier tip about writing characters you know. Draw from your unique background to add interesting elements to the people who populate your world. If you're black, do not set out to write a book about the black experience. Write a book that will engage your readers, then weave in personal experiences that will put them in your shoes.

Brokeback Mountain is a great movie because it's a great movie... not because it's about gay cowboys. *Thelma and Louise* works because it's exciting, not because it's a statement about feminism. *Chariots of Fire* is about a group of Christians, but the action in the movie transcends Christian values.

You know the ironic part? When you push a cause to the background of your story, it'll shine more brilliantly than if you made it the subject of the whole book. By keeping your readers hooked in a good plot and interesting characters, they'll be moved by your hidden cause. And who knows, your exciting novel might attract people who oppose your stance!

If your goal is to attract a niche market, then ignore this rule. There are plenty of novels that are successful in small communities, but more often than not, they read like boring propaganda and rarely expand to a mainstream audience.

DON'T ROMANTICIZE THE STRUGGLE

Yes, there are many infamous writers who struggled with the writing process from Franz Kafka and Kurt Vonnegut to Aaron Sorkin and Dan Harmon. They have talked extensively about writer's block, procrastination, and absolute hatred of their own work... but using them as the rule instead of the exception *romanticizes the struggle.*

You don't need to be tortured to be a good writer. You don't need to experience darkness to write honestly about it. You don't need to be suicidal like Virginia Woolf or Ernest Hemingway. You may doubt your work (you WILL doubt your work), but you don't need to condemn it. Writer's block is a problem to overcome, NOT a necessary part of the process. Learn the difference between DEALING with the struggle and REVELING in it.

At the end of the day, those famous writers who hated to write *were still producing work.* Are you?

LEARN THE RULES, THEN BREAK THEM

This applies to all forms of art, but especially writing.

Compared to computer programers, lawyers, doctors, and engineers, authors don't have THAT many things they need to remember in order to do their job well. Once you've nailed the basics, you need to stop reading about the craft and PRACTICE it.

If you want to be a proficient writer, you need to treat how-to books as a starting point for your brain. Use the concepts you've mastered here as a mental spring-board to develop your own voice. Read enough how-to books to understand the craft completely, practice the craft until it becomes second nature, then practice again and again and again until *you write your own rules*. This is how you stand above the rest.

EXPERIENCE MATTERS

Life experience is the soil for great ideas. It permeates the author's work in the form of rich anecdotes, nuanced characters, and honest drama. But experience doesn't come overnight. It takes *years* to cultivate.

This DOES NOT mean you can't start writing when you're young. You don't need to have extensive life experience to master every writing tool under "Extremely Simple Tips," "Advanced Concepts," or "Developing Useful Habits." Those lessons can be learned at any age... so start now!

Drama, Discovery, Darkness, Catharsis, and Truth, however, are concepts that develop with experience.

So get out of the house. Travel alone. Travel with a friend. Fall in love. Get your heart broken. Consume media that challenges you. Put yourself in surreal situations. Face your fears in the most literal ways. Eat what grosses you out. Make new friends. Don't "people watch" at airports; people watch at *funerals*. Email self-published authors and ask to be a beta reader. Discuss politics with someone who's views you despise. If you don't have kids, babysit. Take a graphic design class. Teach yourself a skill you never thought you'd use. Join the the local theater. Volunteer. Take jobs that put you face-to-face with art of any kind.

And most importantly, *take notes*.

Although life experience is essential to your work, the good news is *you're getting better every day.*

WRITING IS HARD

Sometimes it seems like everybody wants to be a writer. The job is romantic. It lures hordes of teens and adults with the promise of fame, prestige, and money. Everyone has great ideas. Everyone lives exciting lives that would make great stories. Everyone has the first ten pages of The Great American Novel buried in their nightstand drawer. Besides, writing can't be *that* hard, can it? If you can read a book, you can write one... right?

Writing fiction requires a very specific set of skills that—if you believe the right-brain/left-brain dynamic—don't often overlap. Here's a non-comprehensive list of skills you'll need to finish a full-length novel:

-An active imagination
-A mastery of language including vocabulary and grammar
-The ability to organize your thoughts in a cohesive manner
-The self-discipline to sit at your desk and work for hours at a time
-An understanding of subtext
-At least some interest in the human condition
-Enough self-awareness to know what's working and what isn't
-A Valyrian steel backbone

If you're self-publishing, the list grows longer:

-Graphic design skills for covers
-Web design skills for websites
-Marketing skills
-Social skills to communicate with beta readers and fans
-A basic understanding of Search Engine Optimization

-Thick skin for the onslaught of criticism
-Devastating self-awareness at every stage of the process

But that's not all! You'll also need:

-Time to write
-Money for test books, promotional books, advertising, and caffeine
-A community of readers willing to give feedback
-Steady employment that doesn't leave you drained when it's time to write
-Copious amounts of luck

Even if we accomplish everything on this list, some of us will still go years without a positive review... and the majority will never make enough money to live on.

There are people out there working every single day toward achieving YOUR dream. Are you working as hard as they are?

THE UNSTOPPABLE VOICE OF DOUBT

The voice in your head is true. You're not good enough. You'll never make it. You're a terrible writer. Stop NOW before you embarrass yourself any further!

...

You're still here? That didn't scare you away? Then you might be a real artist.

I'm ending this book on a downer. I could make the last chapter super encouraging (God knows I'd get better reviews) but that wouldn't be TRUTH, would it?

Successful writers doubt themselves... *always.* The doubt usually manifests itself as a tiny voice telling them they suck. But successful writers learn to ignore the voice. They write anyway. *They forge on.* They read constantly, not just for fun, but to dissect the words, structure, and characters to better understand how each device works. They carry a notebook with them at all times because they're terrified they'll hear an interesting anecdote and forget it. Many of the rules in this book came naturally to them; they were already learning from TV, texting like they write, and pondering the meaning of truth because *that's how their brains work.* They sit for hours in front of a screen until words form sentences and sentences form chapters and chapters form books. They don't talk about the great idea they had for a new novel... *they write the damn novel.* Successful writers don't write for fame. They don't write for money. *They write because they don't have a choice.*

If this is you, chase your dream to the end.

The voice in your head will say you're going to fail. The voice will say you're garbage. The voice will say other writers are better and this book won't help and you're wasting your precious time.

So re-read the section called *"Writing is Hard."* Scan the list of skills you'll need to become a successful writer. Then ask yourself in all seriousness... do you have what it takes?

Because the voice never goes away.

DID YOU LIKE THIS BOOK?

Please take a minute to rate and review it.

Reviewing books on sites like Amazon and Goodreads is vital to the success of self-published authors. Not only does every rating make our work more visible to potential readers, honest feedback is often our only source of motivation to continue doing what we love.

So if you like a book—*any book*—show your support with a friendly review.

OTHER BOOKS BY JAKE VANDER ARK

The Accidental Siren

Mara Lynn is the most beautiful girl in the world. James Parker is the
ordinary boy who discovers her power. Set in 1994, "The Accidental
Siren" depicts the joys and consequences of young love as Mara and
James meet, shoot a movie, fend off bullies, and explore the potential of
infinite beauty.

The Brandywine Prophet

Suburban life has turned William Carmel from a drug-fueled prodigy
into a gentle husband and father. When the voice of God commands him
to construct a million-dollar theater on the hill behind his home, the
budding prophet obeys and unleashes his dormant madness and savage
creations on his family and town.

Lighthouse Nights

Jules and Trevor take advantage of suicidal teens by encouraging them
and profiting off their deaths. When Jules falls in love with their eighth
target, she's forced to make a series of life-or-death decisions and a
single, impossible change.

Fallout Dreams

Ava Lane wants to overcome her fear in peace. Mia wants to party. The
twins reach their breaking point when they move into an isolated house
in the middle of the Arkansas woods. As Ava moves from accepting her
fear to relishing it... as Mia exploits a tragedy to impress her new
friends... the man hiding in the cellar watches their every move.

The Day I Wore Purple

Jonathon and Gavin Nightly are in love with Hannah Lasker, a gifted
artist on the verge of a meltdown. Their lives spiral toward heartbreak
with the release of a controversial vaccine that grants eternal life.

Made in the USA
Lexington, KY
14 November 2017